piano | vocal | guitar

TOM PETTY and the HEARTBREAKERS MOJO

MOJO

Photography by Sam Jones

ISBN 978-1-4234-9866-7

HAL•LEONARD® CORPORATION

7777 W. BLUEMOUND RD. P.O. BOX 13819 MILWAUKEE, WI 53213

JEFFERSON JERICHO BLUES

Words and Music by
TOM PETTY

Mid - night creep - in' ____ out to the
But in my sec - ond mind I knew it was
sit ____ here think - in', ____ my thoughts will ____

ser - vant's shack. ____
time to go. ____
o - ver - flow. ____

If I

Kept a se - cret un - der the bed, ___
Yeah, and I still ___ get ___ nerv - ous ___
And I can't ___ keep ___ from ___ cry'n', ___

___ wrapped in a bur - lap ___ sack.
___ ev - 'ry time that bu - gle ___ blows.
___ can't keep time from ___ mov - in' ___ slow.

Well, I

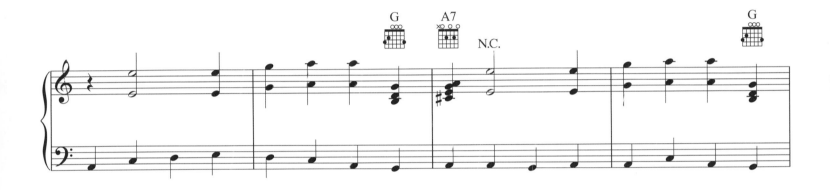

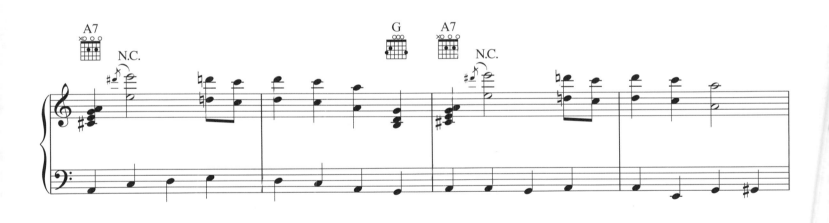

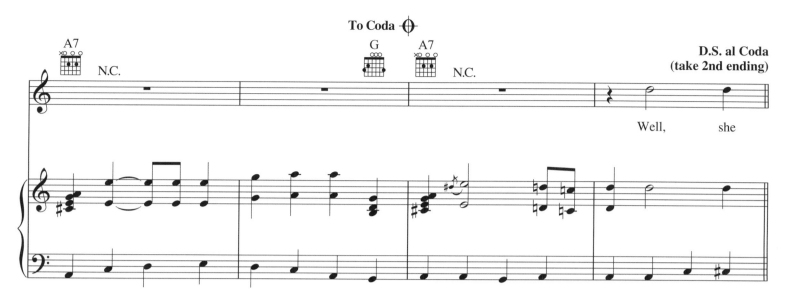

Well, she

FIRST FLASH OF FREEDOM

Words and Music by TOM PETTY
and MIKE CAMPBELL

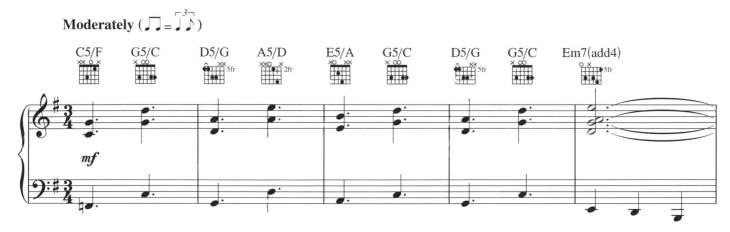

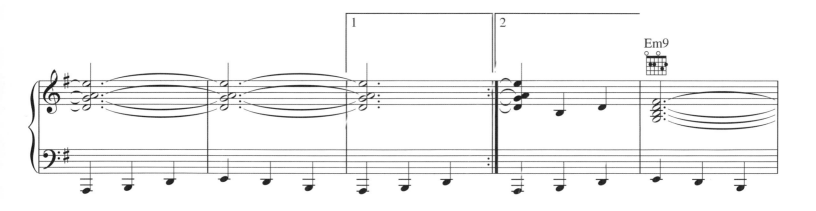

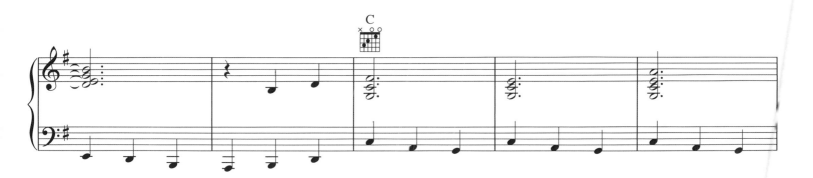

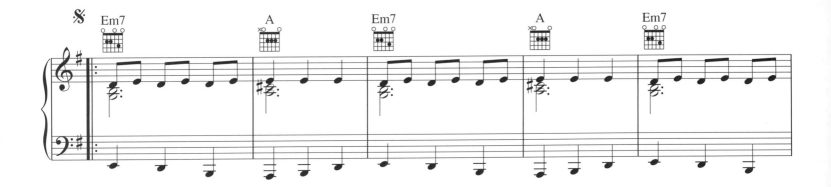

On our first flash of free - dom, I
A fist full of glo - ry, a
Down ev - 'ry can - yon and

called out your name. ___
suit - case of sin, ___
moun - tain we fall ___

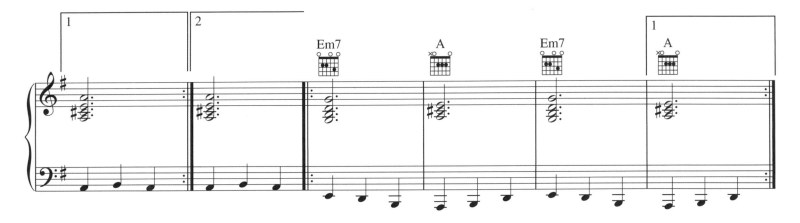

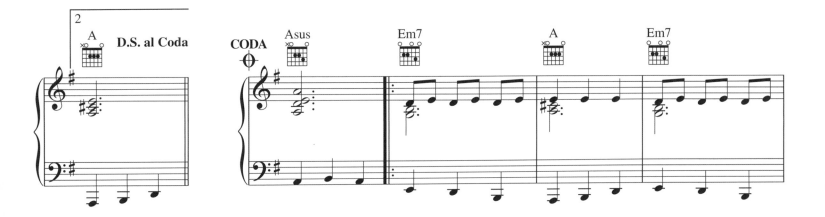

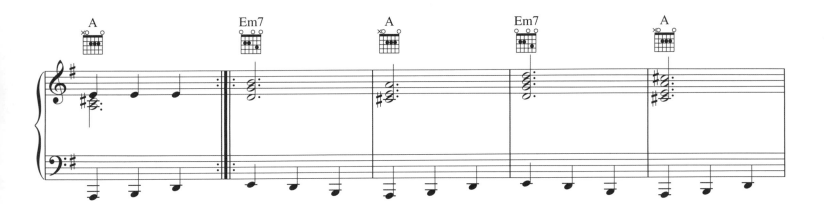

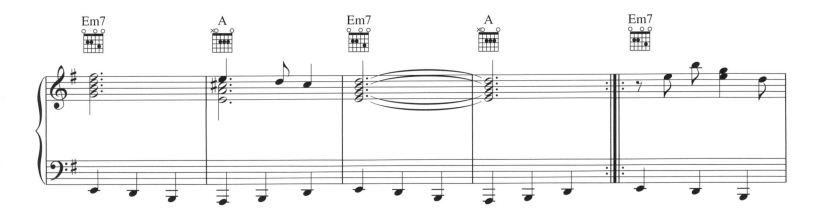

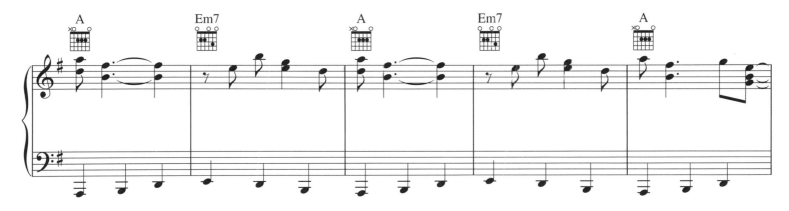

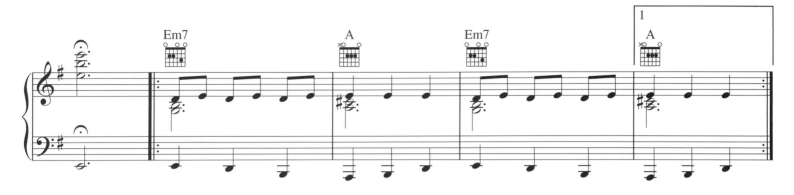

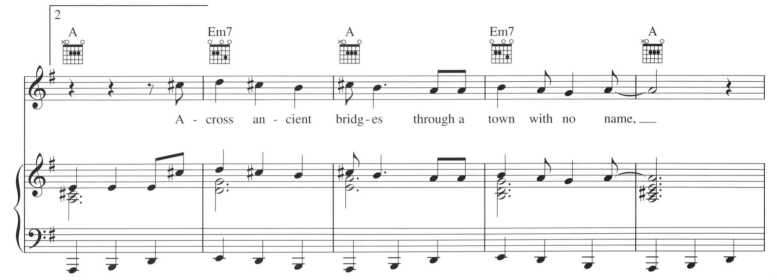

Across ancient bridg-es through a town with no name, ___

a - cross paint-ed ___

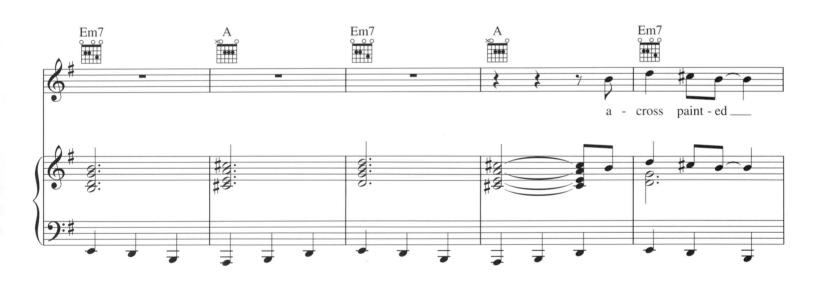

hills that no rich man can claim, ___

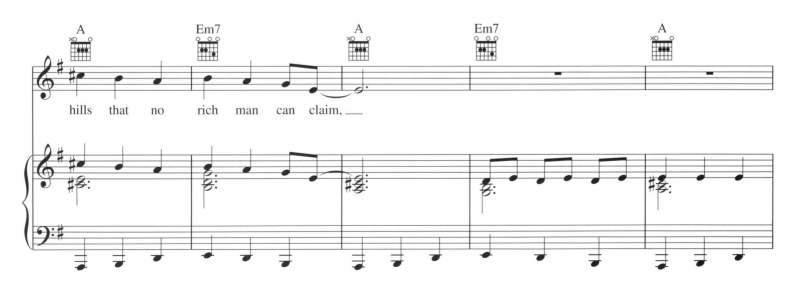

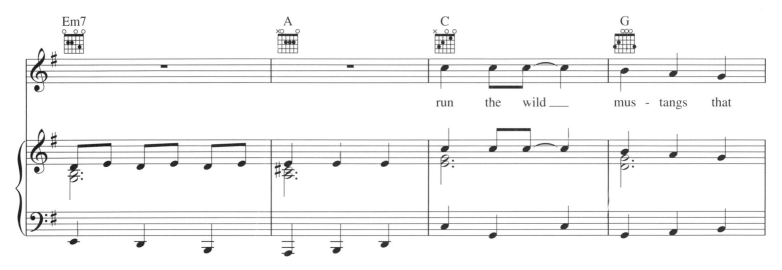

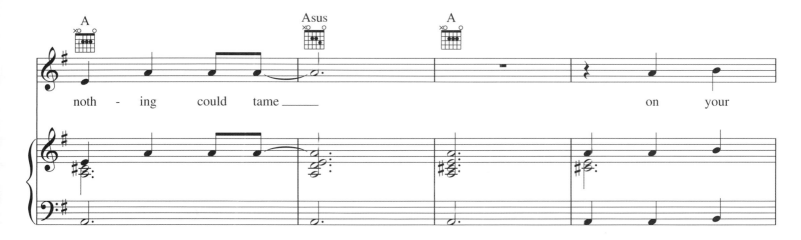

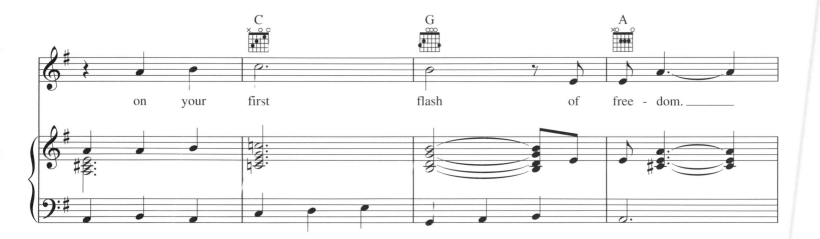

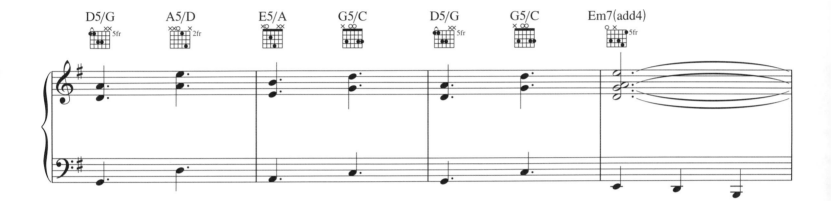

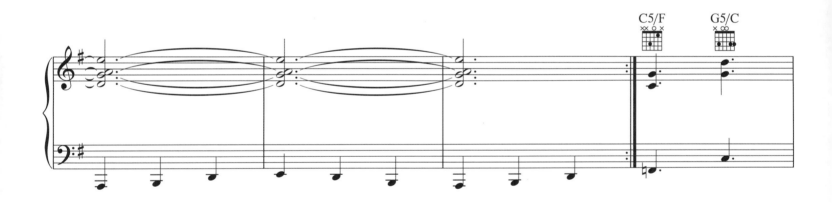

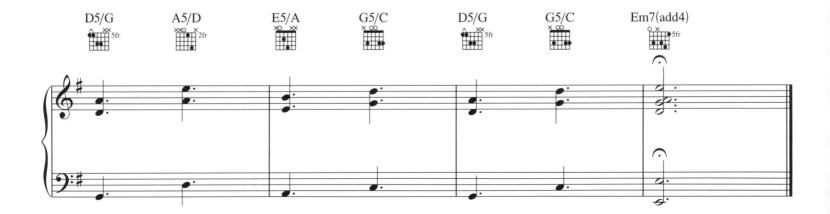

RUNNING MAN'S BIBLE

Words and Music by
TOM PETTY

Moderately fast

Play 3 times

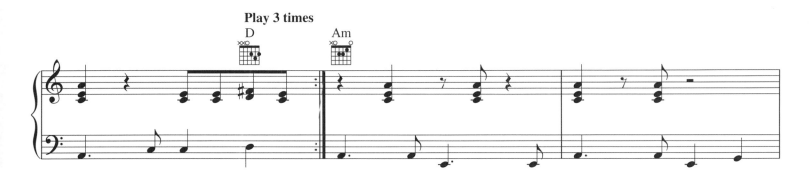

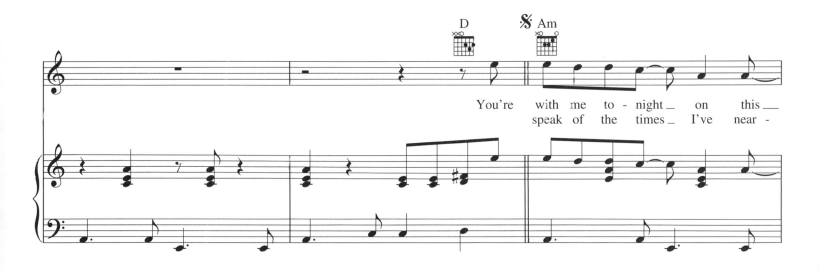

You're with me to-night __ on this __
speak of the times __ I've near -

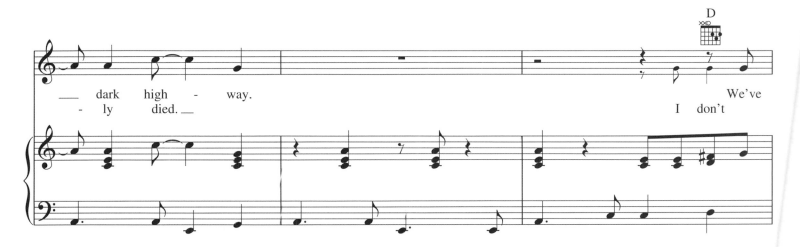

__ dark high - way.
- ly died. __

We've
I don't

run it to-geth - er so ____ man - y times. _
speak of out - last - in' those ___ who are gone, _

We've run it for mon - ey, we've run it for mu - sic.
or the things I've __ done __ I care not to re - mem - ber,

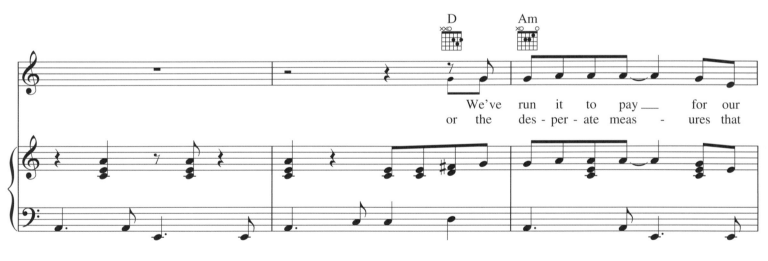

We've run it to pay __ for our
or the des - per - ate meas - ures that

in - no - cent crimes.
might have been wrong.

I
(3.) Hon - ey,

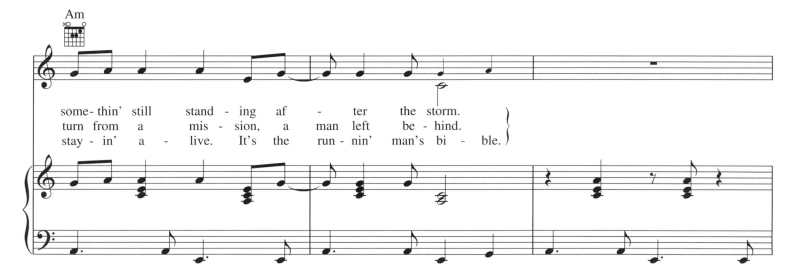

some- thin' still stand - ing af - ter the storm.
turn from a mis - sion, a man left be - hind.
stay - in' a - live. It's the run - nin' man's bi - ble.

Here's __ one to glo - ry ____

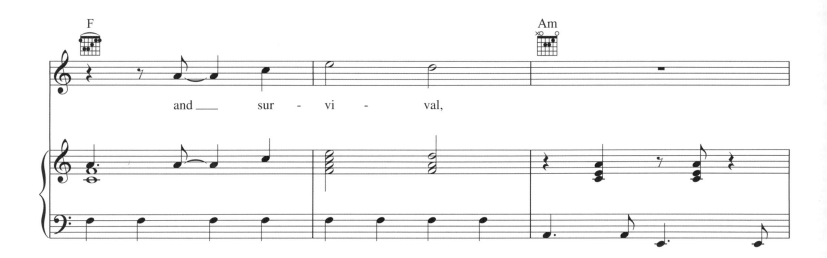

and ___ sur - vi - val,

and stay - in' a - live. _____ It's the run - ning man's

bi - ble, yeah. _____

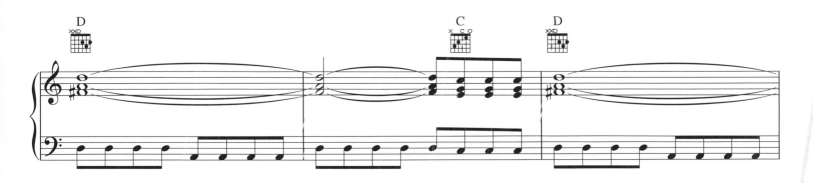

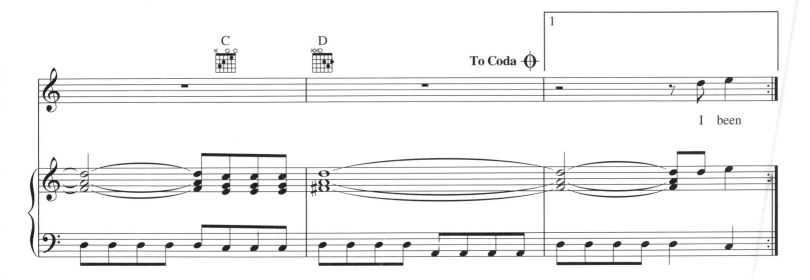

To Coda ⊕

1

I been

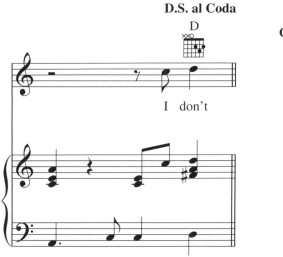

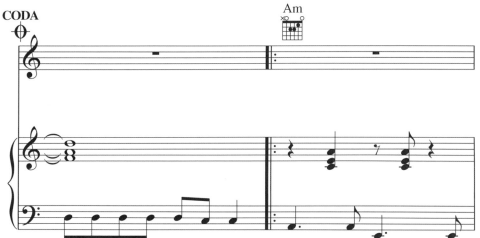

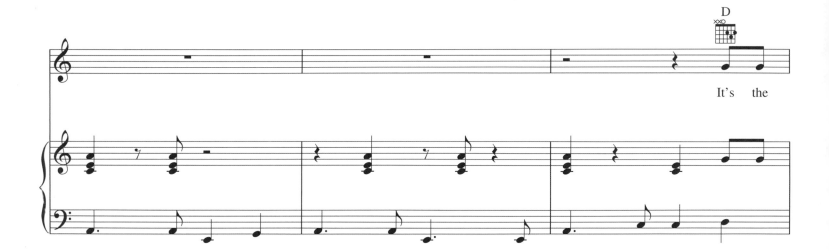

run - nin' man's bi - ble. _____

It's the run - nin' man's bi - ble. _____

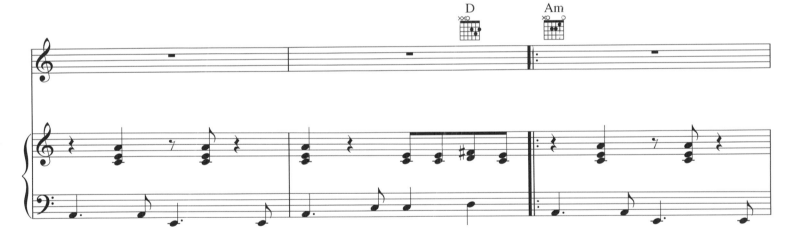

THE TRIP TO PIRATE'S COVE

Words and Music by
TOM PETTY

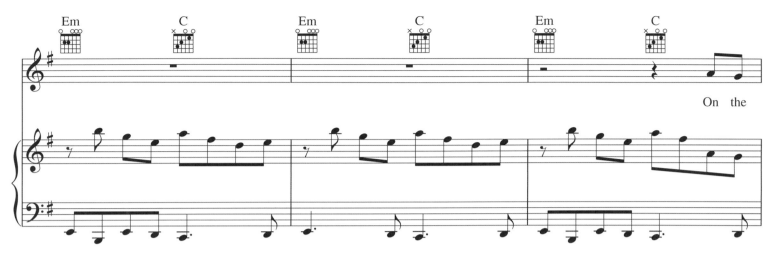

On the

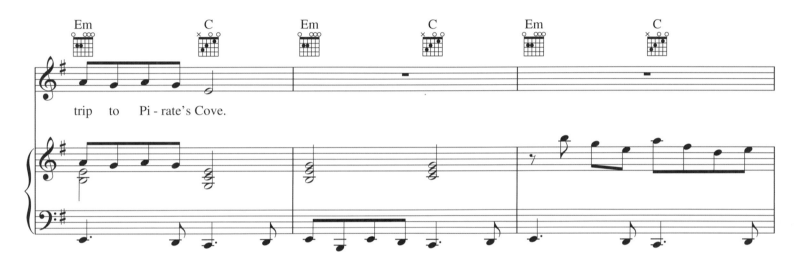

trip to Pi - rate's Cove.

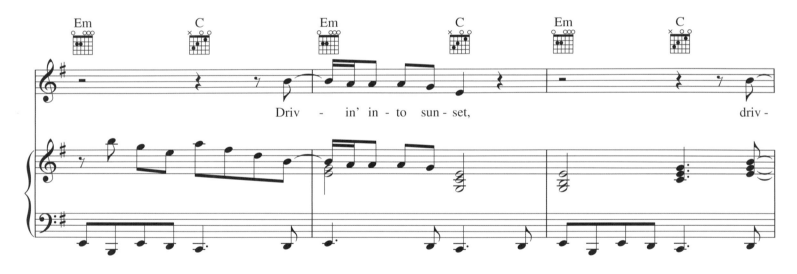

Driv - in' in - to sun - set, driv -

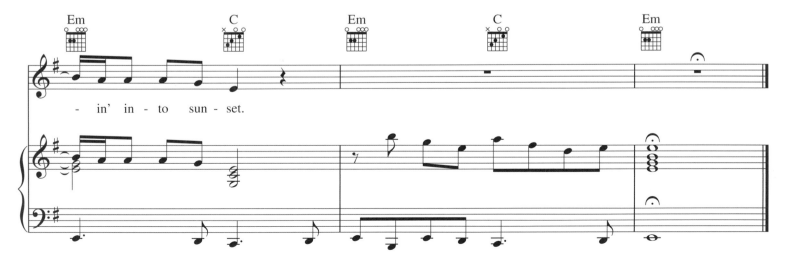

- in' in - to sun - set.

CANDY

Words and Music by
TOM PETTY

(1.,4.) I sure like ___ that can - dy.
(2.) don't drink co - ca co - la,
(3.) don't much ___ like walk - in',

I don't go _____ for them tur - nip greens. ___
but I sure _____ like the ol' moon - shine. ___
but I love my El - do - ra - do ride. _____

Well, I
I ain't

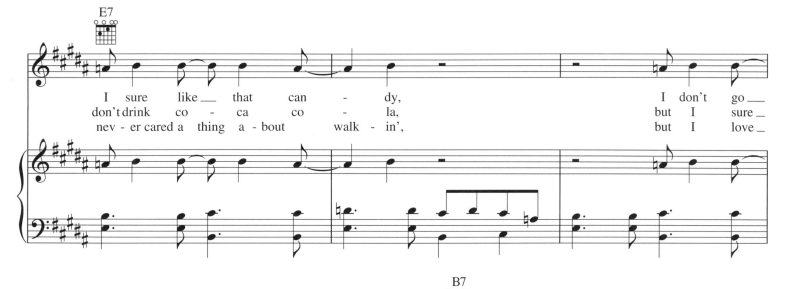

I sure like ___ that can - dy,
don't drink co - ca co - la,
nev - er cared a thing a - bout walk - in',

I don't go ___
but I sure ___
but I love ___

___ for them tur - nip greens. ___
___ like the ol' moon - shine. ___
___ my El - do - ra - do ride. ___

So, when you
Yeah, we
Yeah, we

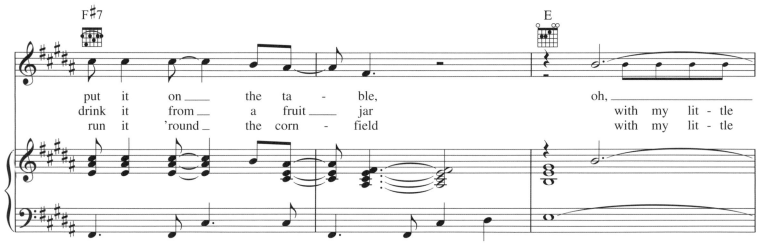

put it on ___ the ta - ble,
drink it from ___ a fruit ___ jar
run it 'round ___ the corn - field

oh, ___
with my lit - tle
with my lit - tle

ma - ma, think a - bout me.
ba - by __ by __ my side.
ba - by __ by __ my side.

2. Well, I
3. Well, I

I sure like __ that can - dy, I sure like __ that can -

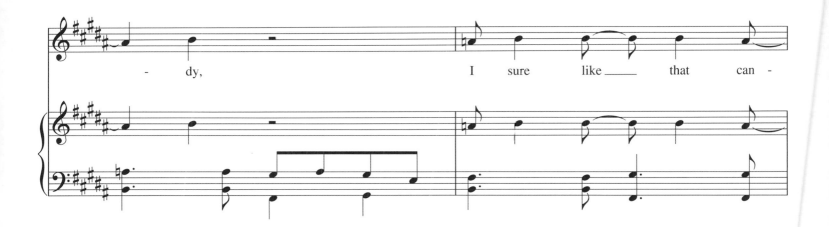

- dy, I sure like ____ that can -

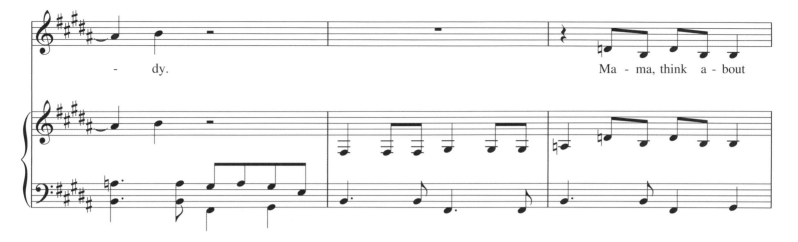

- dy.   Ma - ma, think a - bout

me.

Ma - ma, think a - bout   me.

B5

NO REASON TO CRY

Words and Music by
TOM PETTY

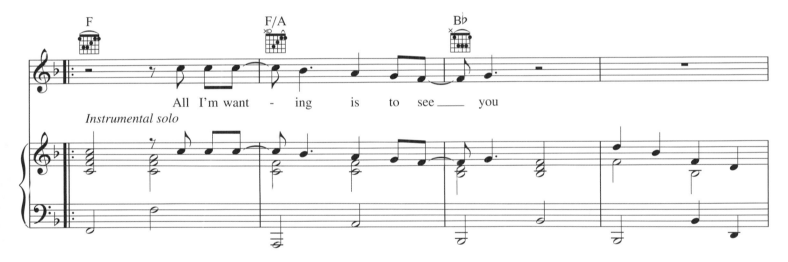

All I'm want - ing is to see ____ you

Instrumental solo

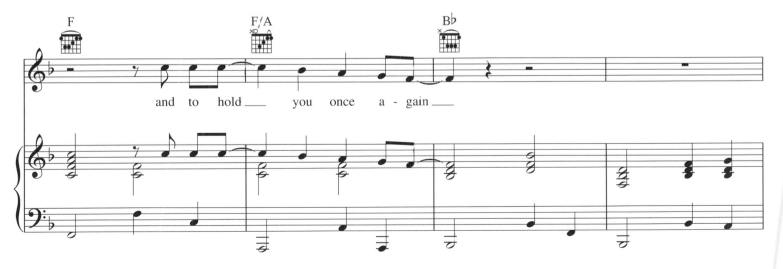

and to hold ____ you once a - gain ____

and see the sun co-lor___ your hair___

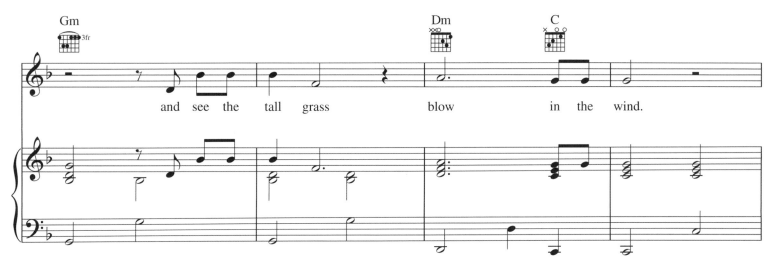

and see the tall grass blow in the wind.

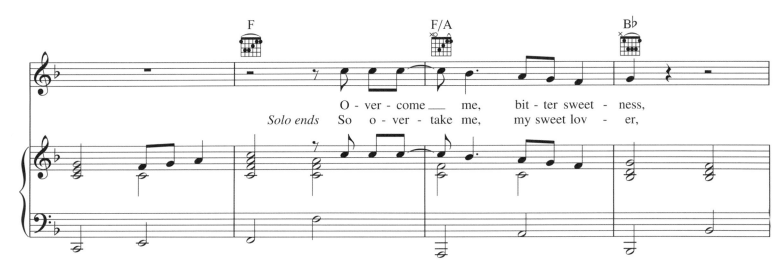

O - ver - come ___ me, bit - ter sweet - ness,
Solo ends So o - ver - take me, my sweet lov - er,

put me un - der a mag - ic spell.
let me kiss ___ your ___ hon - ey lips.

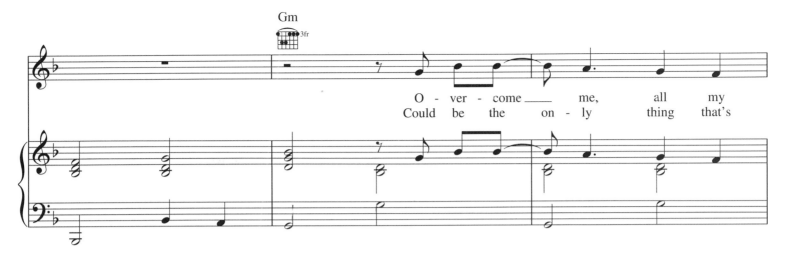

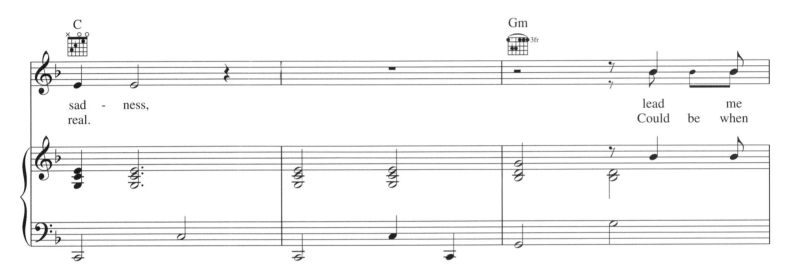

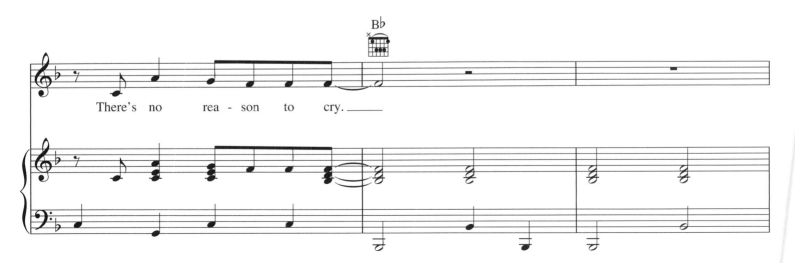

There's no rea-son to cry. ____

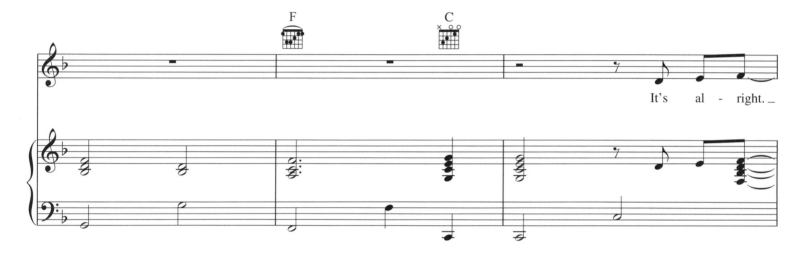

It's al - right. _

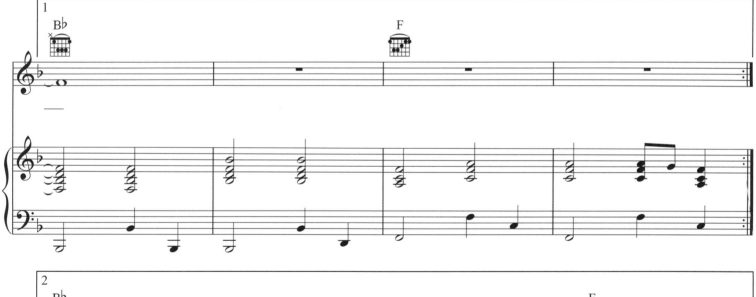

I SHOULD HAVE KNOWN IT

Words and Music by TOM PETTY
and MIKE CAMPBELL

Leave it to you _____ to
It was all _____ right there _____ in

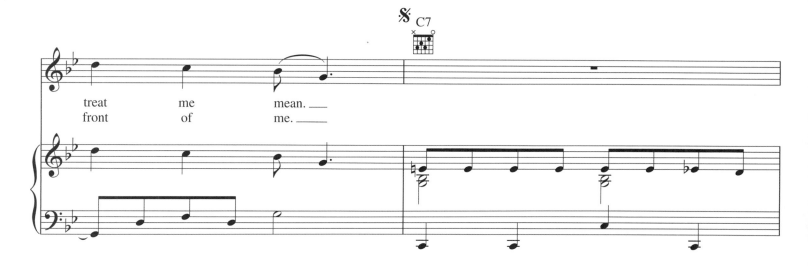

treat me mean. _____
front of me. _____

Ev - 'ry prom - ise
Sold down the riv - er,

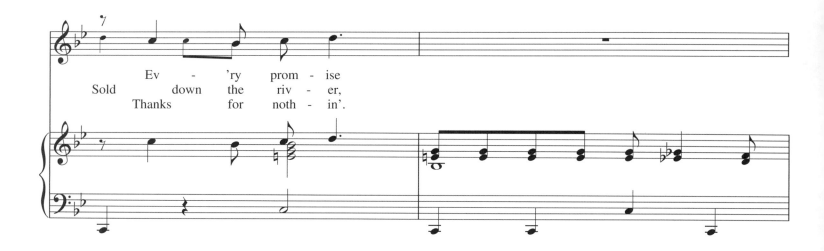

was just a run - a - round.
left _____ for dead. _____
Yeah, thanks a lot. _____

Thanks for noth - in'.

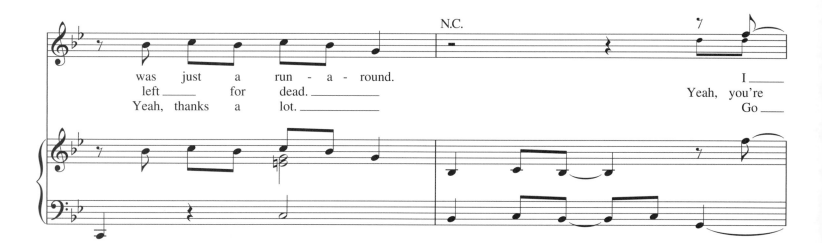

I _____
Yeah, you're
Go _____

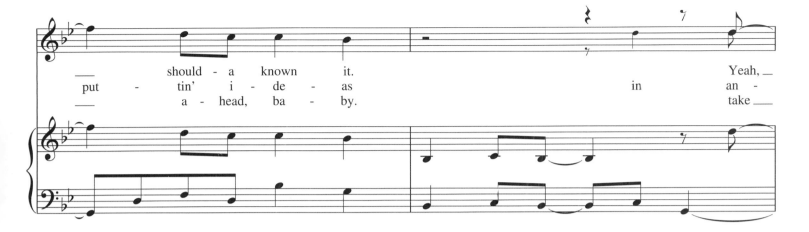

should-a known it.
put - tin' i - de - as
a - head, ba - by.

Yeah,
in an -
take

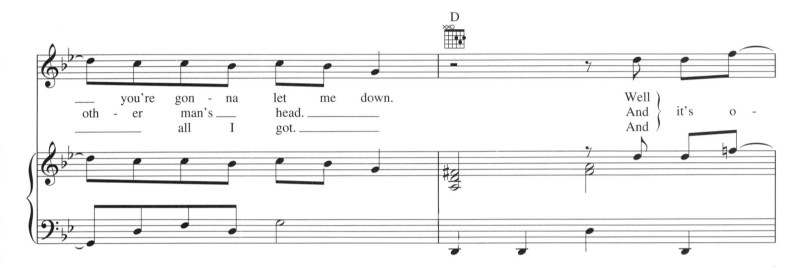

you're gon - na let me down.
oth - er man's head.
all I got.

Well
And
And

it's o -

D

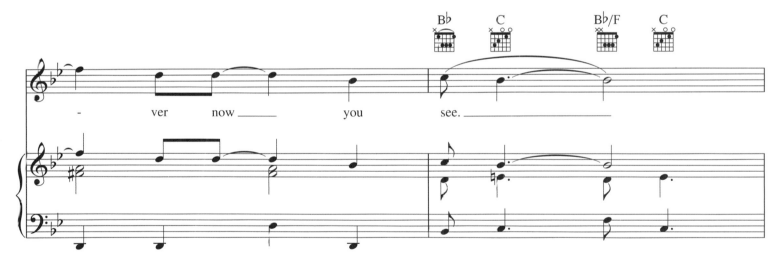

- ver now you see.

Bb C Bb/F C

Bb C

N.C.

To Coda

A tempo

It's the

last time you're gon - na hurt me. _____

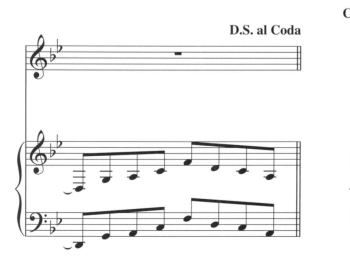

D.S. al Coda

CODA

It's the

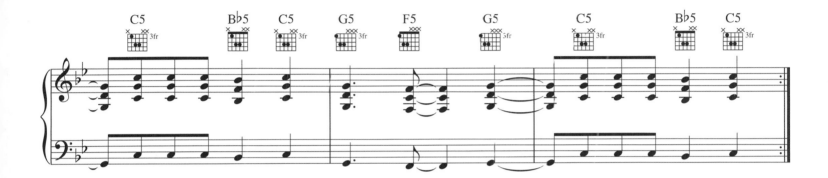

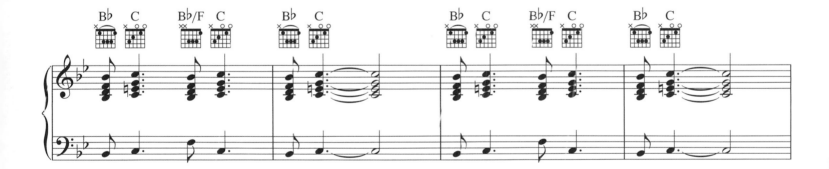

U.S. 41

Words and Music by
TOM PETTY

Moderately fast

My dad-dy came __ a march-in' o-ver the hill __ at dawn. __

Had to make that wage, man. That's how we got a - long.

My dad - dy's life was work - in',

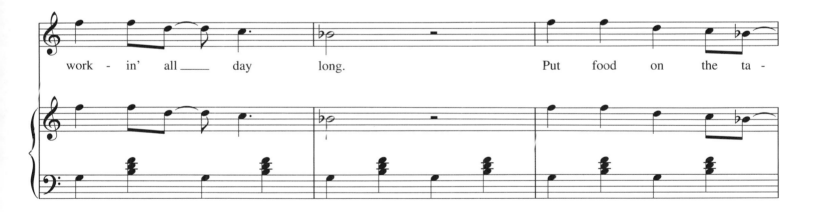

work - in' all day long. Put food on the ta -

- ble, and the chil - dren sang a song, yes, the chil -

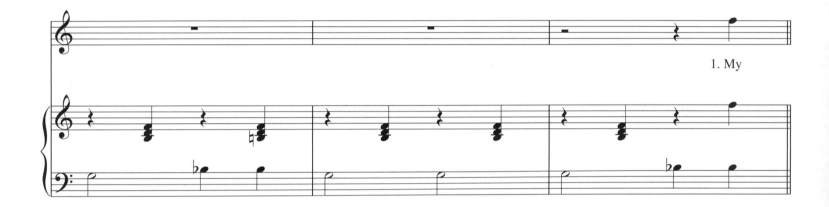

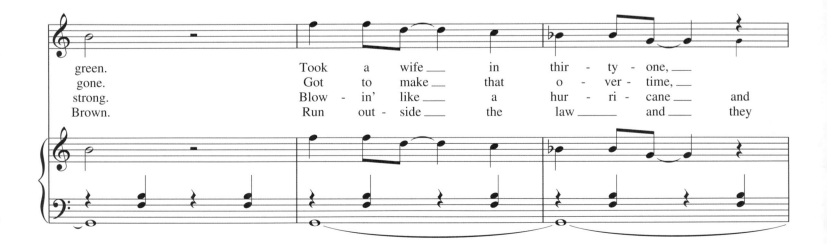

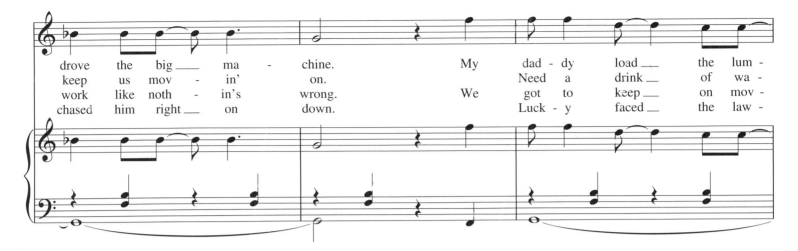

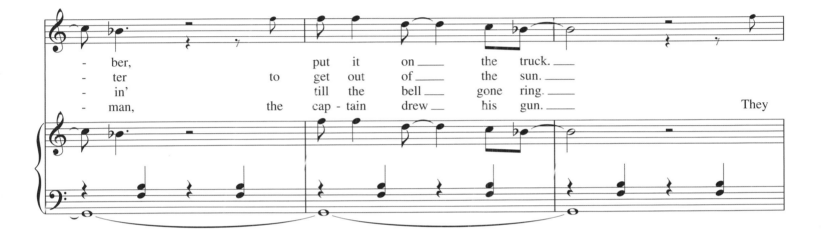

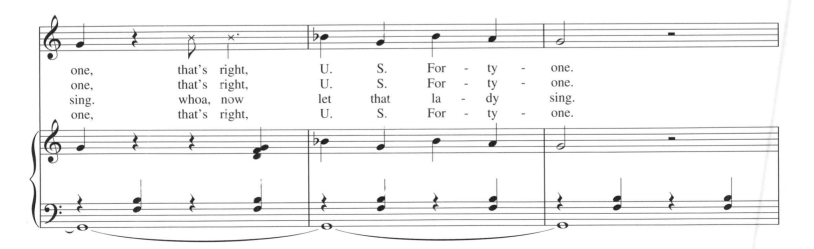

1-3

2. Well,
3. The
4. His

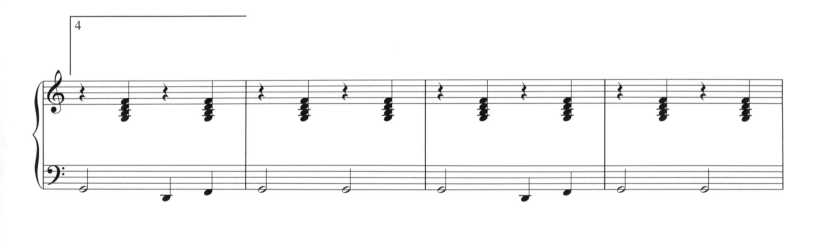

4

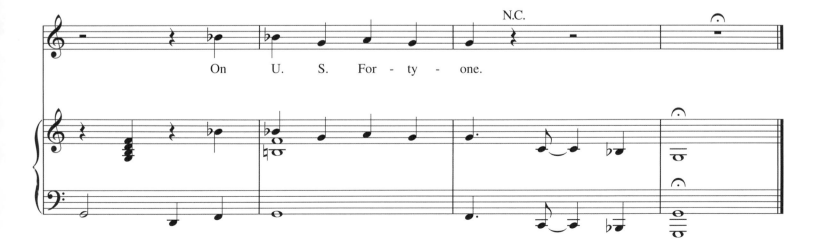

On U. S. For - ty - one.

N.C.

TAKIN' MY TIME

Words and Music by
TOM PETTY

hon - ey, my fuse____ was lit._____
what's on the road_ af - ter me.____

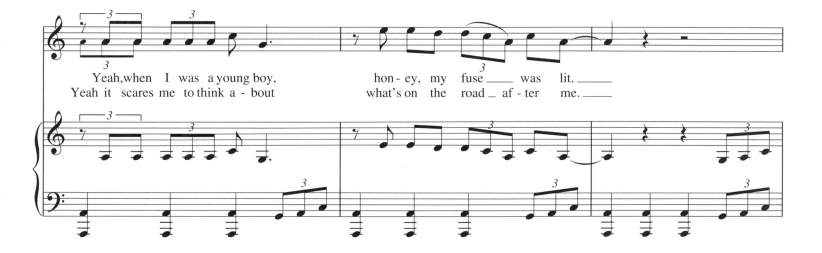

Yeah, when I was a young boy,
Yeah it scares me to think a - bout

hon - ey, my fuse____ was lit.____
what's on the road_ af - ter me.____

A   G

N.C.

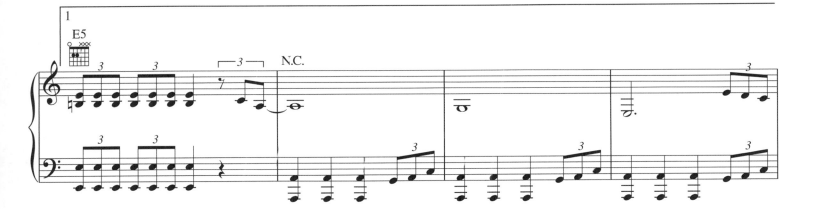

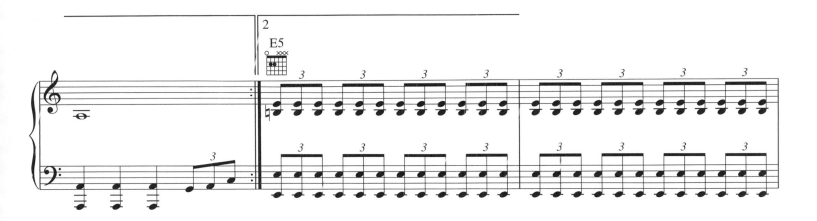

LET YOURSELF GO

Words and Music by
TOM PETTY

might not   get here for   three or four   days.
Brings a bag of rec - ords and she plays 'em till   dawn.
Man, she was a beau - ty in   six - ty -   nine,

Got to make a lit - tle bit   go a long   way.
Give me lit - tle lov - in' then she got to go   home.
but there ain't __ no __ more __ com - in' down __ the   line.

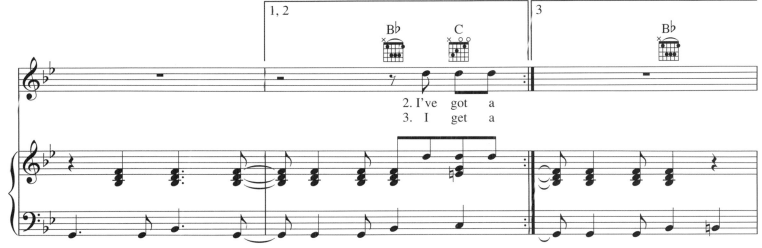

2. I've got a
3. I get a

When times are hard, _____ when you start feel - in'

low, ___ let your - self go. ___

When the riv - er's ris -

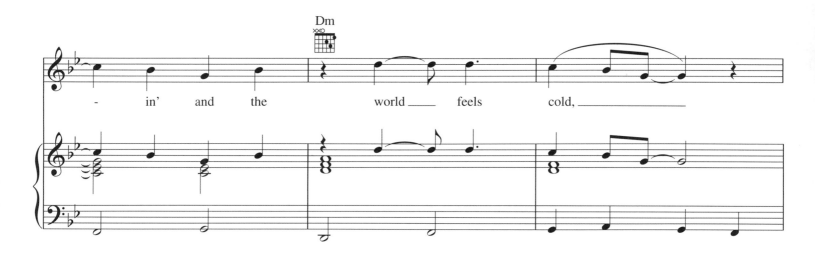

- in' and the world ___ feels cold, ___

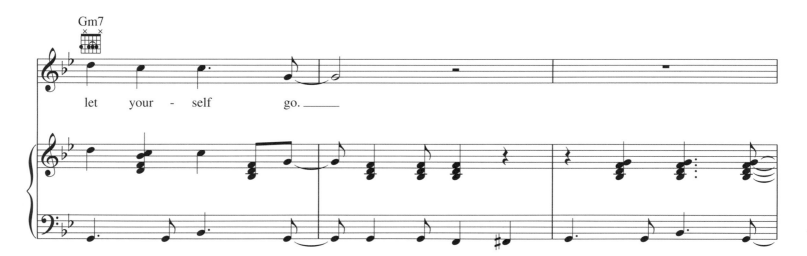

let your - self go. ___

Hon - ey let your - self go. ___

To Coda ⊕

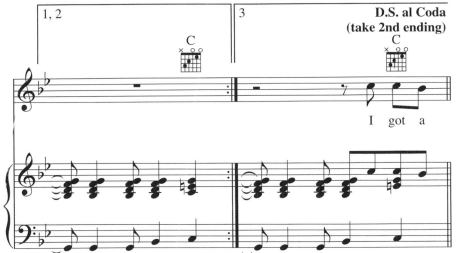

I got a

D.S. al Coda
(take 2nd ending)

CODA ⊕

Let your - self go. ___

Repeat and Fade | **Optional Ending**

DON'T PULL ME OVER

Words and Music by
TOM PETTY

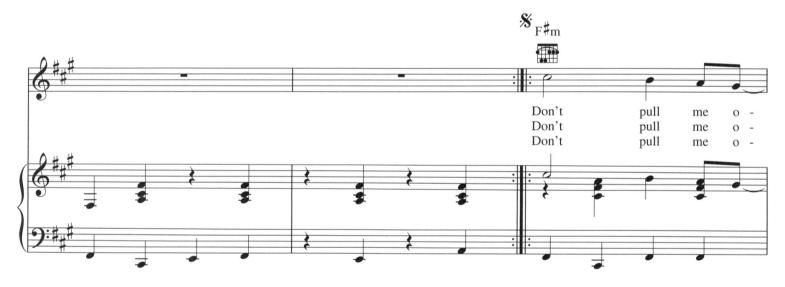

Don't pull me o - ver,
Don't pull me o - ver.
Don't pull me o - ver.

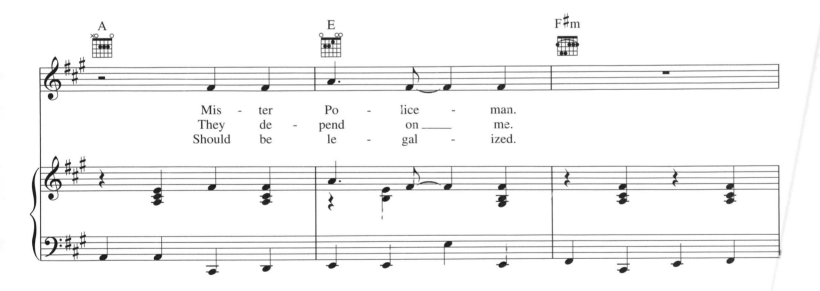

Mis - ter Po - lice - man.
They de - pend on ___ me.
Should be le - gal - ized.

To Coda

What I've got to do ___ won't hurt an - y -
What I've got to say ___ won't hurt an - y -

one. ___
one. ___
Where I've
What I've

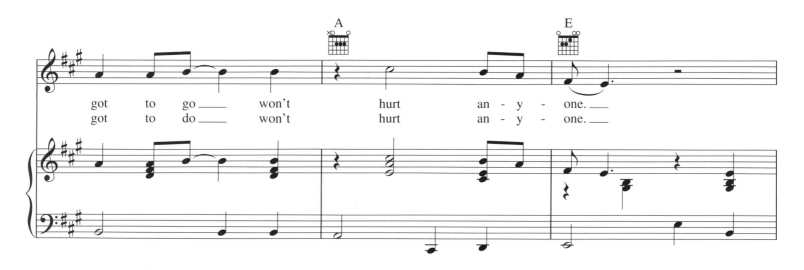

got to go ___ won't hurt an - y - one. ___
got to do ___ won't hurt an - y - one. ___

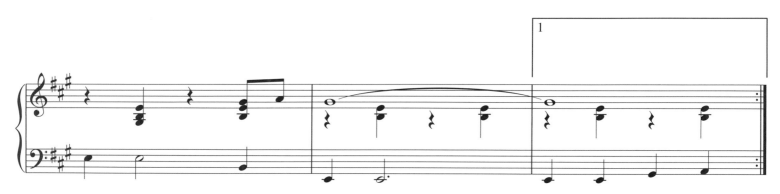

When the moon - light

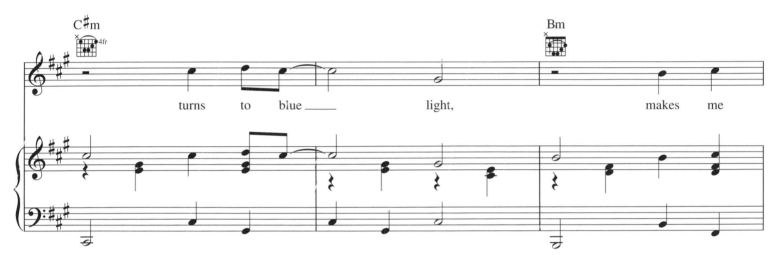

turns to blue _____ light, makes me

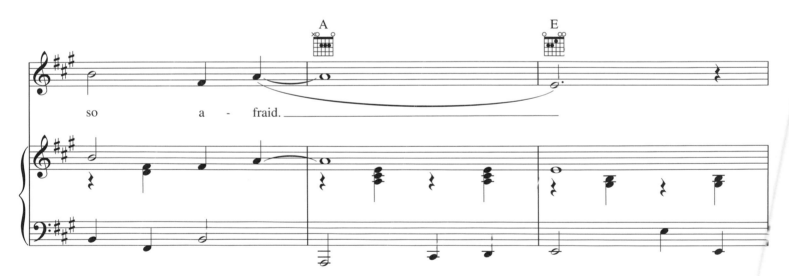

so a - fraid. _____

So let me go, _____ leave me 'lone _

'til   I'm   home   and

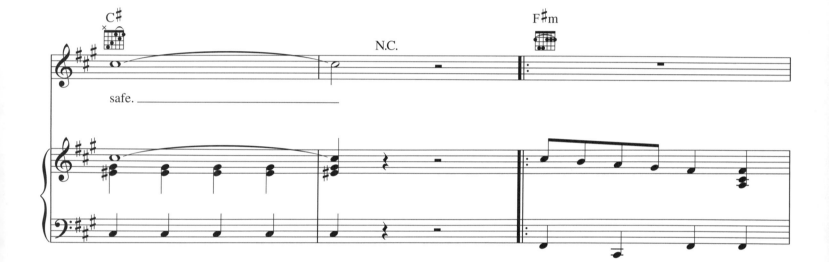

safe. _____

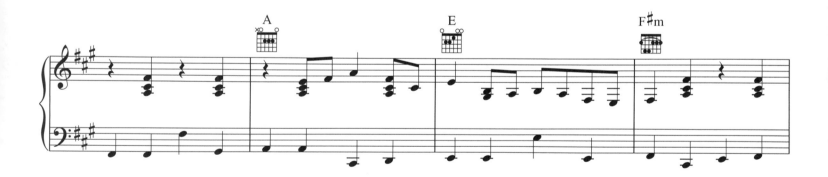

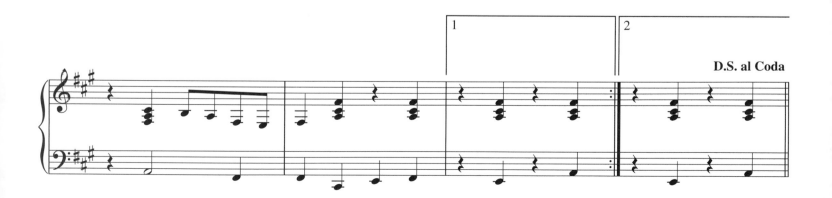

D.S. al Coda

Don't pull me o - ver, Mis - ter Po - lice - man.

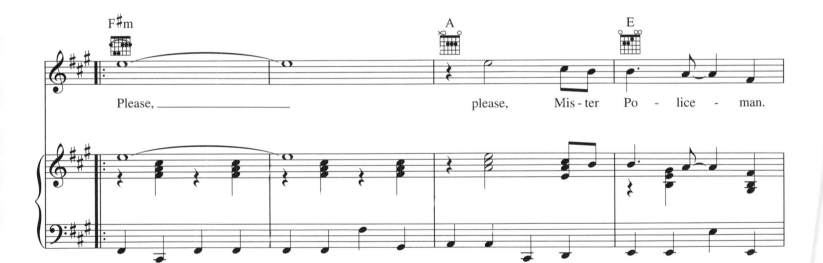

Please, _____ please, Mis - ter Po - lice - man.

LOVER'S TOUCH

Words and Music by
TOM PETTY

Hard __ liv - in'

kill - ing me. __ I need that wom - an

to set me free. __

F5   Eb/Ab   F5   Eb5

F5   F5   Eb/Ab   F5   Eb5   F5

And I want her,   I want her so much __

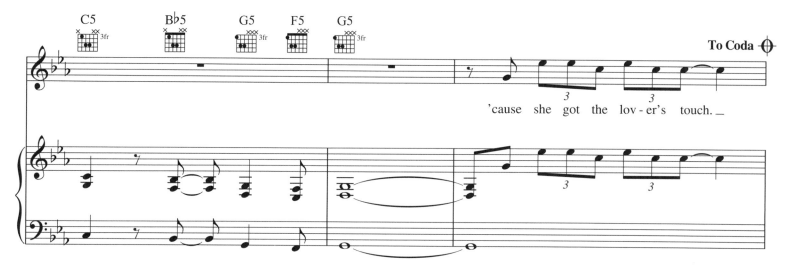

To Coda

'cause she got the lov-er's touch. __

Feel sold out, __
Instrumental solo ad lib.

wa-ter get-tin' high - er.

Liv-in' on the shore-line,

star- in' at the fire. _____

2

Solo ends   I hear her voice

when I'm all a - lone. _____   Gives me com - fort, _____

D.S. al Coda

so   soft _____ and low.

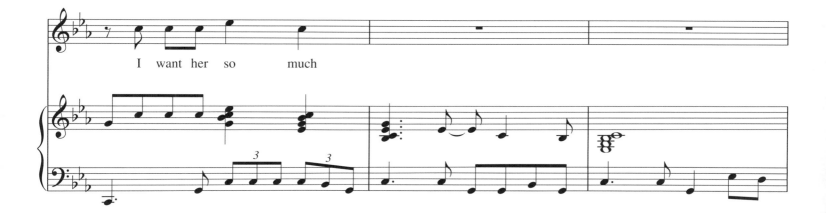

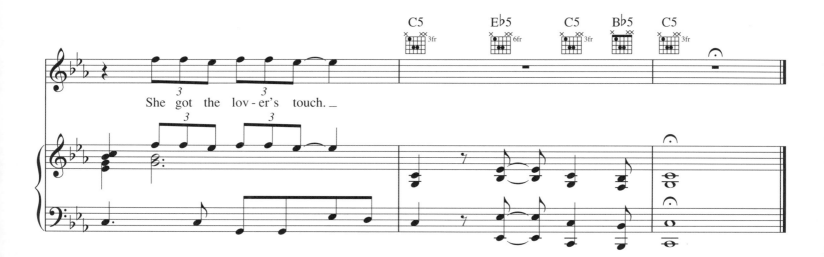

HIGH IN THE MORNING

Words and Music by
TOM PETTY

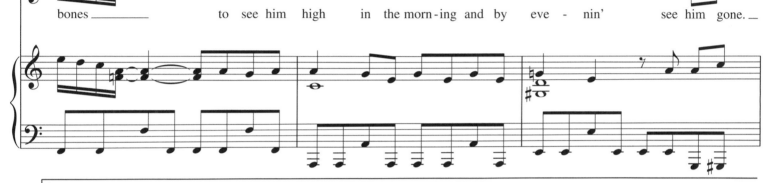

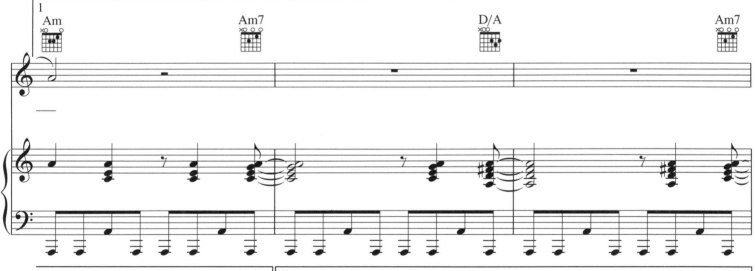

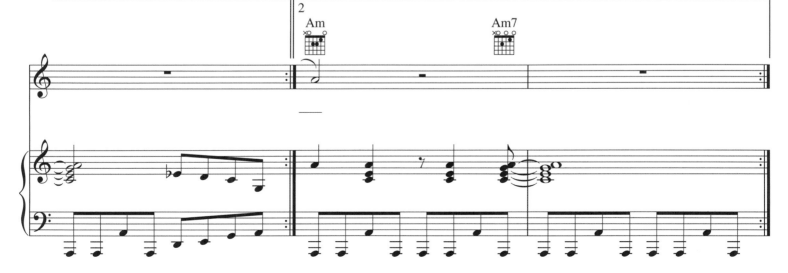

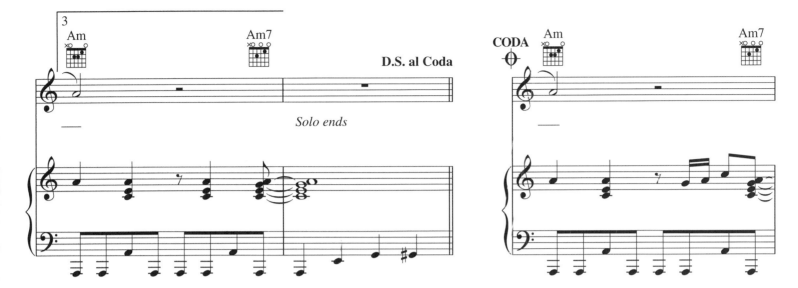

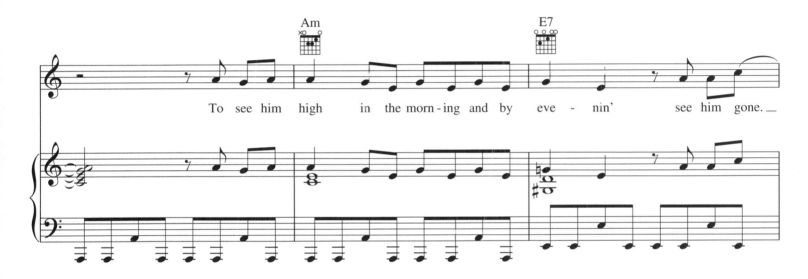

To see him high in the morn-ing and by eve-nin' see him gone.

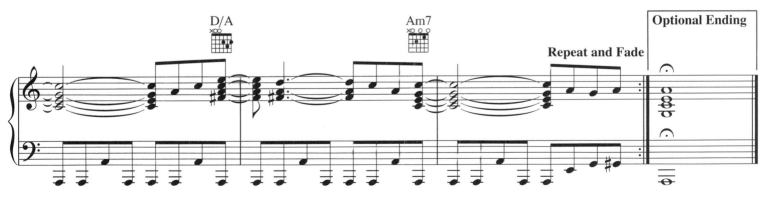

SOMETHING GOOD COMING

Words and Music by
TOM PETTY

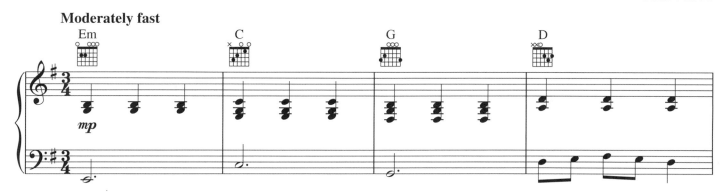

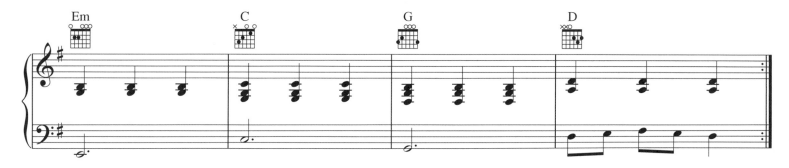

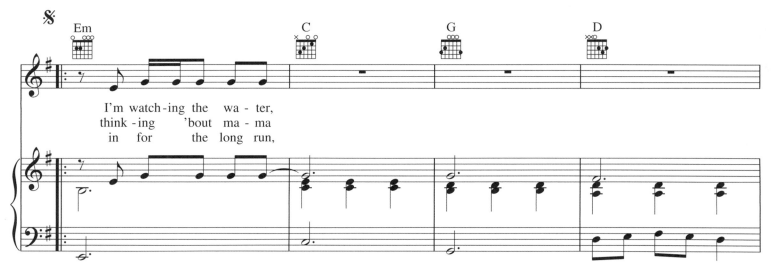

I'm watch-ing the wa- ter,
think- ing 'bout ma - ma
in for the long run,

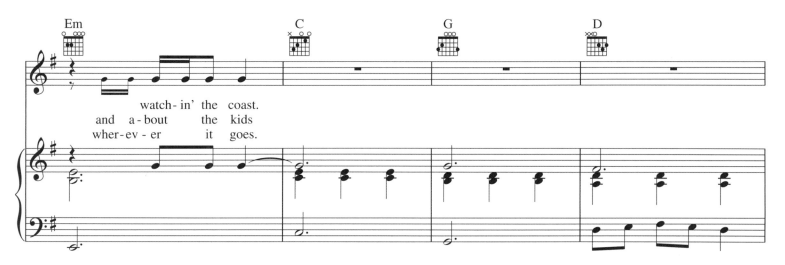

watch- in' the coast.
and a-bout the kids
wher-ev - er it goes.

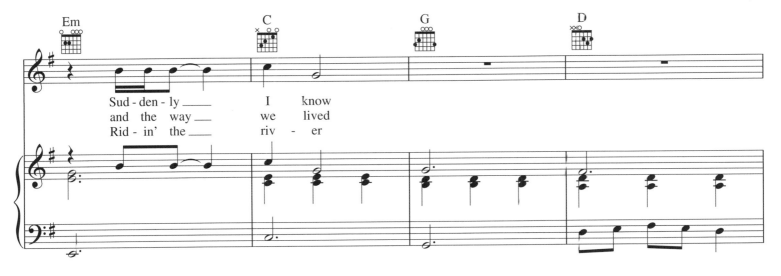

Sud - den - ly ____ I know
and the way ___ we lived
Rid - in' the ___ riv - er

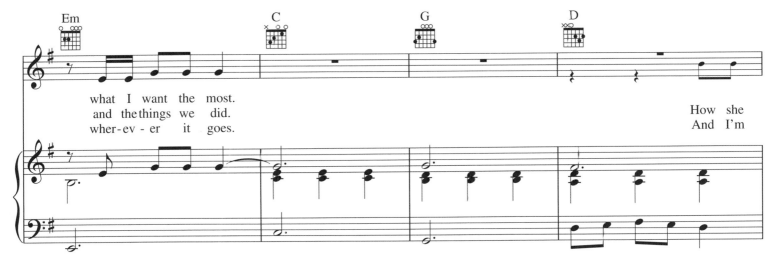

what I want the most.
and the things we did.
wher-ev - er it goes.

How she
And I'm

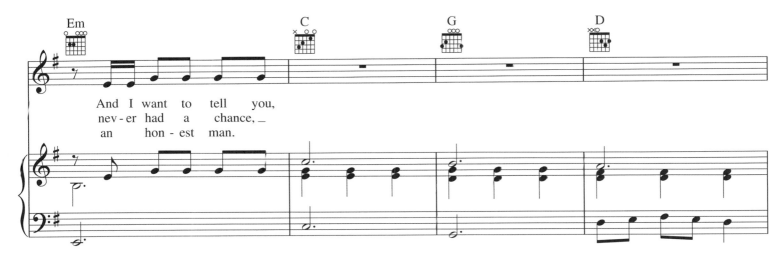

And I want to tell you,
nev - er had a chance, __
an hon - est man.

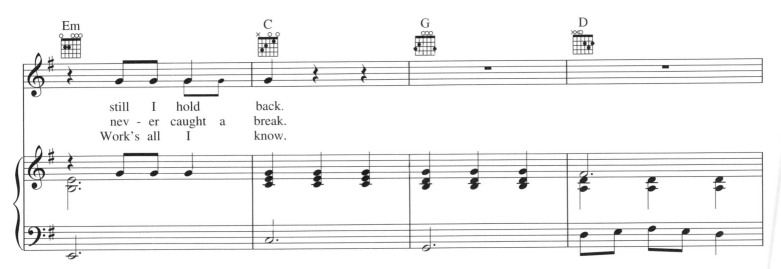

still I hold back.
nev - er caught a break.
Work's all I know.

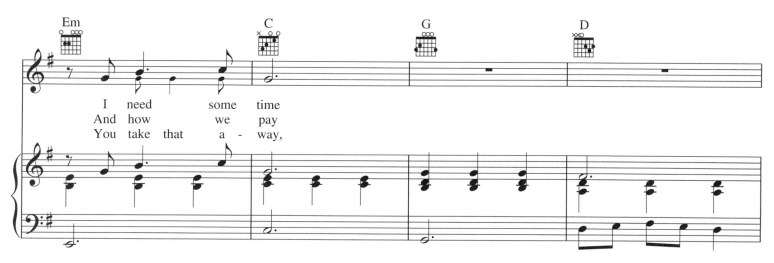

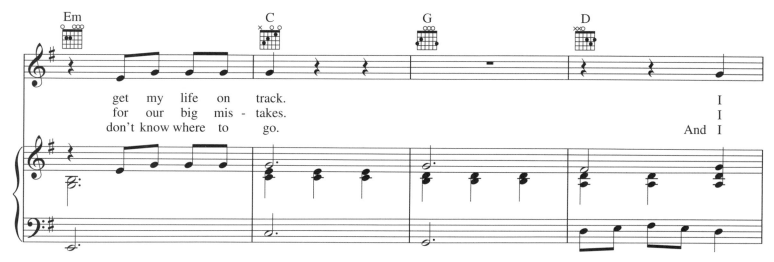

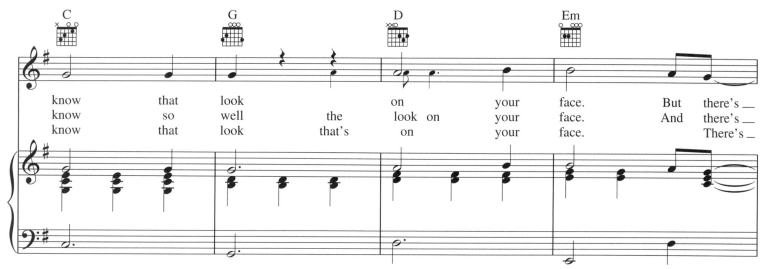

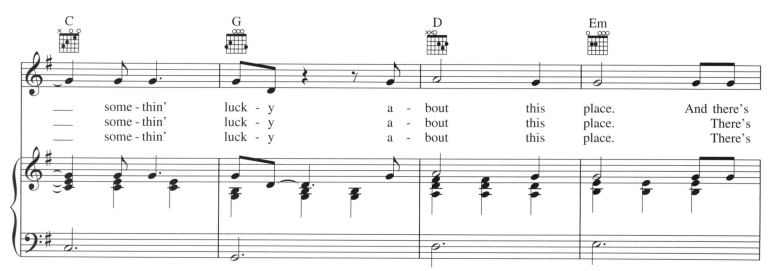

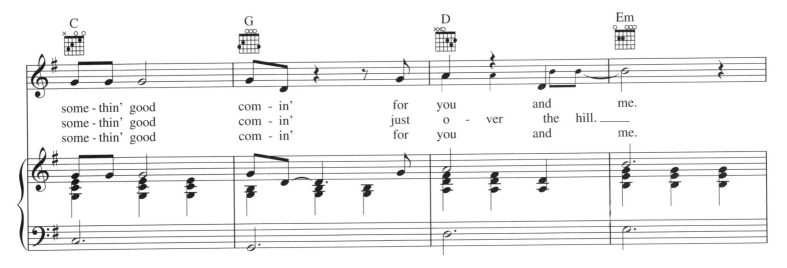

some-thin' good com-in' for you and me.
some-thin' good com-in' just o-ver the hill. _____
some-thin' good com-in' for you and me.

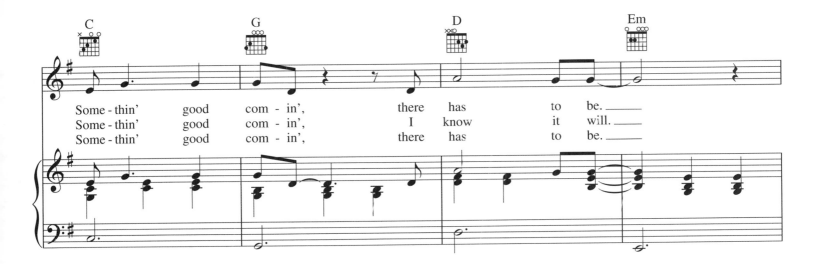

Some-thin' good com-in', there has to be. _____
Some-thin' good com-in', I know it will. _____
Some-thin' good com-in', there has to be. _____

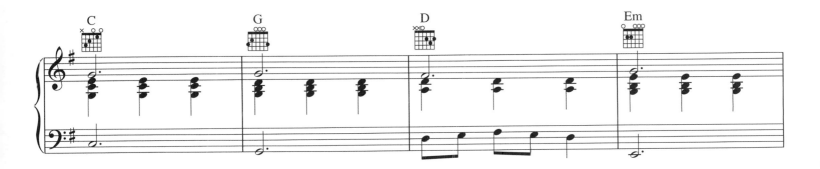

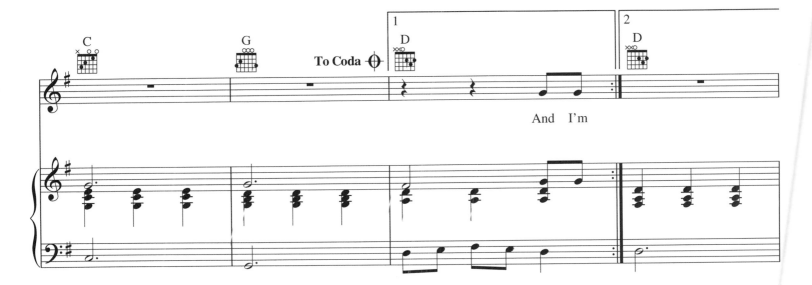

And I'm

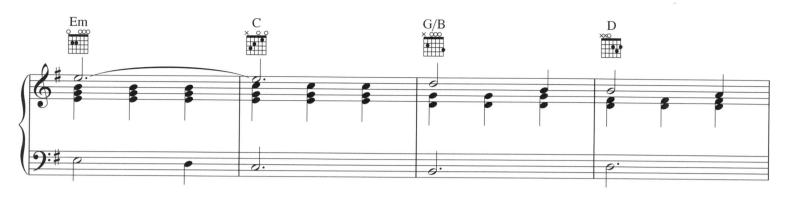

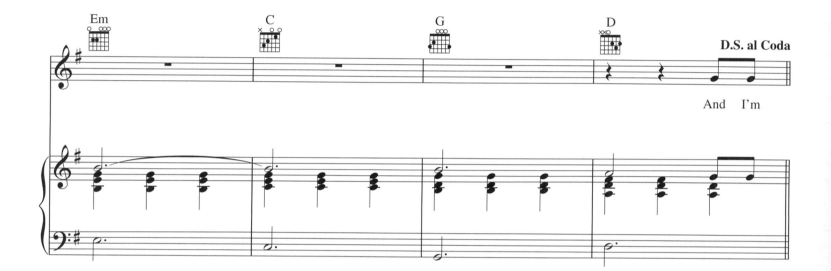

D.S. al Coda

And   I'm

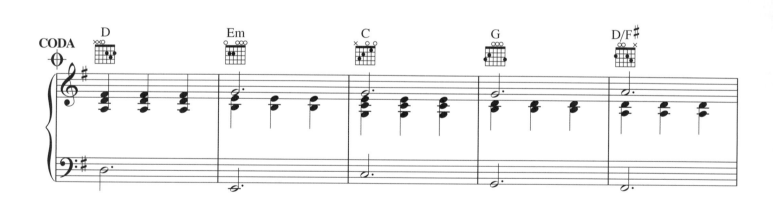

CODA

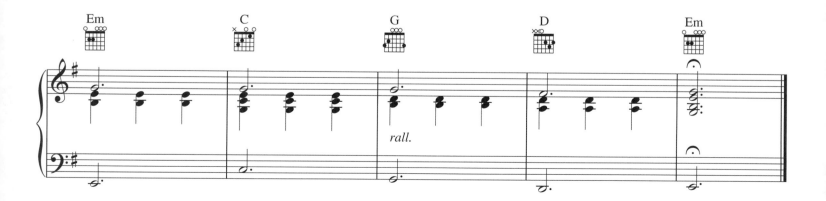

rall.

GOOD ENOUGH

Words and Music by TOM PETTY
and MIKE CAMPBELL

Slow Blues feel

She was hell   on her ma-ma,

im - pos - si - ble to please.   She wore out   her dad - dy.

Got the best of me. And there's some-thin' a-bout her

that on-ly I can see and that's good e-nough.

You're bare-foot in the grass

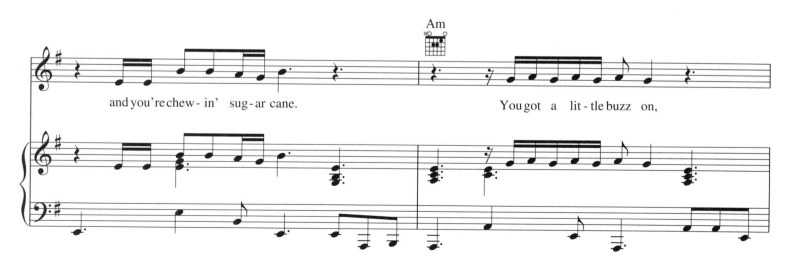

and you're chew-in' sug-ar cane. You got a lit-tle buzz on,

Good e-nough for me, ___

good e-nough for right now,   yeah. ___

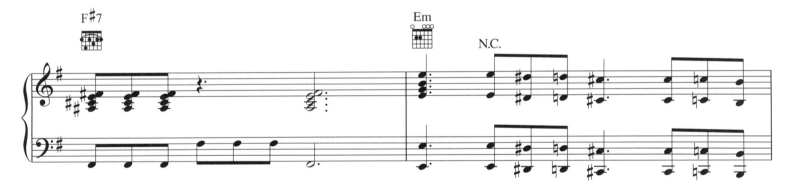

God bless this land.

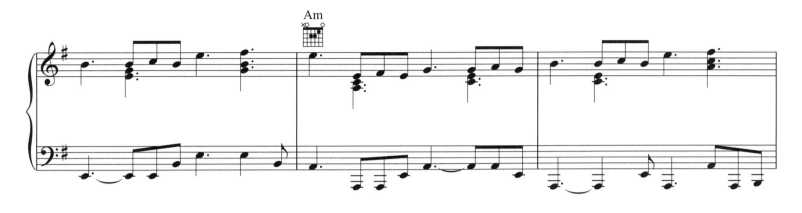

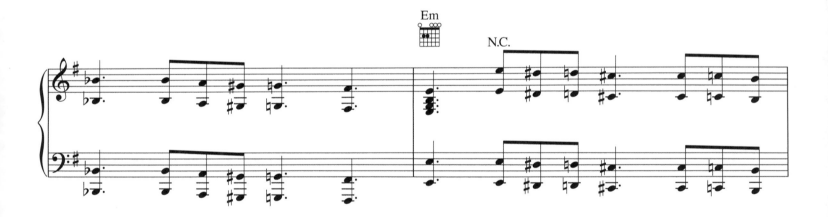